Chincoteague Revisited

A Sojourn to the Chincoteague and Assateague Islands

Chincoteague Revisited

A Sojourn to the Chincoteague and Assateague Islands

Photography by Dorothy Camagna
Essays by Jennifer Cording

Foreword by Jim Clark

The Oaklea Press

Richmond, Virginia

Pages ii–iii: *Children explore the wonders of a clam bed as the midsummer sun sets over Little Toms Cove.*

Page iv–v: *Houses on the Assateague Channel near Birch Town provide striking views of water and marshland.*

Page vi–vii: *An aerial view of Chincoteague Island on a hazy, late summer day. The Assateague and Chincoteague channels flank the island, as the mainland stretches into the distance.*

We wish to acknowledge and thank the following for their contributions to this project.

Kirk Mariner's *Once Upon an Island: The History of Chincoteague,* Miona Publications, New Church, Virginia, 1996.

William H. Amos's, "A Barrier Island Natural History" in *A Guide to Assateague Island National Seashore, Maryland and Virginia.* (Handbook 106). Produced by the Division of Publications, National Park Service, U.S. Dept. of Interior, Washington, D.C., 1985 (reprinted 1999).

Chincoteague National Wildlife Refuge Website: *http://chinco.fws.gov*

ISBN 1-892538-11-3 (hardcover)

LCCN 2003109442

The Oaklea Press
6912-B Three Chopt Road
Richmond, Virginia 23226
http://www.OakleaPress.com, email: Orders@OakleaPress.com
Telephone: 1-800-295-4066, Fax: 1-804-281-5686

This book is dedicated to the memory of my mother and grandmother.

Dorothy Camagna

Blake Cove and Blake Point on Chincoteague Bay protect the North Main Street community from rough water. A tidal flat extends into the bay in the background.

The Bay Breeze, *a charter sailboat, faces Chincoteague's swing-span bridge.*

Foreword

Photographers strive to compose images that depict a strong sense of place. They want the viewer to sense the sights, sounds, and atmosphere of a location—to give the viewer the impression of being there. This is no easy task. Writers also attempt to create a sense of place through the use of powerful words. When both images and words are skillfully combined, it is truly a work of art.

Chincoteague Revisited is one of those delightful books that combines beautiful photography with expressive writing to transport the reader to this wonderful island.

Dorothy Camagna's photography celebrates the people, scenery and natural world of Chincoteague, and Jennifer Cording's text provides an enjoyable overview of the island's history, culture and environment. Together, they take us on a delightful journey and create a true sense of place, not only about the Chincoteague community, but other special nearby areas such as the Chincoteague National Wildlife Refuge and Assateague National Seashore.

For those familiar with Chincoteague, either as a life-long resident or a frequent visitor, this book will stir pleasant memories of early morning strolls on the Assateague beach, birding along the tidal channels at Chincoteague National Wildlife Refuge, or taking in a glorious sunset along the island's bayside. For those who have not been tempted by the island, *Chincoteague Revisited* will show why once you visit, you never leave it behind.

Just as the island beckons, *Chincoteague Revisited* will become a gentle reminder that it's time for another visit or two, or three.

Jim Clark
President, North American Nature Photography Association,
photographer and author

Acknowledgments

I would like to thank my husband, Brian, for all his advice, support and patience while I gathered photographs for this book, and especially for his help during the return pony swim, when he paddled a double kayak back to the dock in a torrential downpour, while I snugly nestled under an umbrella protecting my equipment.

I'm grateful to John Schroer for his assistance with obtaining photographs of the wildlife refuge, and to Jay Cherrix and Kelley Jewett for their advice on where to find the best photographic opportunities. Thanks also to all those who provided input regarding the book's content.

I'm also obliged to the many gracious folks who agreed to let me photograph them, particularly Terry Howard, who made a special effort to demonstrate how he and his twin brother, Carey, "wade" clams. Moreover, I wish to thank Linda and Elizabeth Di Fulvio and Jennifer Cording for their patience while I photographed them with their horses.

I'd also like to express my appreciation of the skills of several pilots at Bayland Aviation, who made it possible to amass the aerial photographs. Thanks to the Comfort Suites and Island Property Enterprises for courteous accommodations.

Thanks also to Dodge Color for their prepress services and to Steve Martin at The Oaklea Press.

Dorothy Camagna

I would like to acknowledge the valuable insights of the following people who reviewed the text of *Chincoteague Revisited*: Mark Cording, my husband; Ted Shockley, news editor at the Eastern Shore News, Dr. Miles Barnes, librarian at the Eastern Shore Public Library, Bob and Nancy Conklin, lifelong residents of Chincoteague; John Schroer, manager of Chincoteague National Wildlife Refuge; Mike Hill, Carl Zimmerman and Rachelle Daigneault of Assateague Island National Seashore; and Dr. Kirk Mariner, author of *Once Upon an Island*.

Jennifer Cording

Introduction

During one of my visits to Chincoteague, a friend said, "See you next time the island calls you back." I thought about this farewell as I returned to the mainland over the causeway. I thought about it again a few weeks later, when I felt the need to return—when I heeded the island's call. The compelling allure of the Assateague barrier island and the town not only brought me back for repeated visits, but also beguiled me to represent the spirit and charm of the area in my photography.

I met scores of individuals during the numerous months it took to compile the book, and many suggested places, events or people to photograph. Some took me to locations I hadn't been to before, while others listened or commented as I explored what the book would present. I was encouraged by their enthusiasm to help portray the region's appeal. In pursuit of the photographs, however, I found myself in a few unpredictable situations.

I've long wanted to get aerial shots of the full moon rising over Assateague Island, a photographically difficult feat due to low light levels and the relatively fast shutter speed required for aerial work. In order to capture sufficient light for the shutter speed, the moonrise must take place near sunset, which happens only a few months in any given year. Of course, one also needs obliging weather.

On an evening when the sunset, moonrise, moon phase and predicted clear sky were in concert, I scheduled a Cessna plane for a photo flight. Once near the shoreline of Assateague, however, a low haze materialized on the horizon, delaying the rising full moon's appearance until it emerged from the vapor above the ocean. If overdue by more than fifteen minutes, there would not be enough light.

The pilot positioned the plane so I would face westward for shots of the setting sun. All the while we were buying time, waiting for the moon to rise above the haze. We circled. The sun had set. I scrutinized the eastern sky—still no moon. Just as I was about to give up and head back, a sliver of moon peeked out!

I notified the pilot and pointed. "There's the moon, we've got about five minutes of workable light. Hurry and position the plane so I can face east." The eager pilot did a sharp turn, wings almost vertical, and quickly maneuvered into position. I struggled to keep stomach in check and hands from trembling while taking the last shots of the flight, and made a mental note to never tell a pilot to hurry!

On another shoot, about a week before Pony Penning, I packed my car with long telephoto lens and set out to photograph young foals before they were rounded up. I found a band of ponies that included five mares, the stallion and four foals, all intently grazing in the marsh. Since the horseflies and mosquitoes were particularly bad, I decided to remain in the car and rest the long lens on a beanbag over the car's open window, instead of getting out and setting up the tripod.

I had taken several shots and was engrossed in the next photo's composition, when I noticed the car jerking forward a bit. At first I thought the car moved because I shifted my weight when positioning the long lens, but then I felt the car jerk again, and shortly afterwards heard a gnawing noise. Certainly that wasn't my doing! I turned around to find one mischievous colt biting the corner of the trunk.

I carefully drove ahead, and without the car to intrigue him, the colt trotted toward the other foals. Once off the refuge I checked the damage. The colt had indeed left teeth marks on the trunk. I never repaired the scratches since it seemed like such a unique souvenir of the shoot. And the colt—I consequently bought him at the auction. I always wanted a Chincoteague pony, and circumstances seemed right that this was the pony for me.

I've often wished to photograph the dolphins that seasonally visit the Chincoteague area. I mentioned this to Jay Cherrix, who runs kayak tours near Assateague, and he suggested a jaunt in the Atlantic aboard a double sea kayak. Jay knew where the dolphins gathered and with his help I hoped to photograph them near the surf.

We set off before dawn and were ready to get in the ocean shortly after sunrise. The surf was a bit rough, and Jay suggested we swim the kayak through the surf, then get on once past the breakers. It seemed easy. Jay went into the surf with the double kayak and the paddles, and I followed carrying my camera in protective underwater gear—what amounted to a specially-made plastic tote bag slung over my shoulder.

Swimming beyond the breakers with camera gear in tow was a considerable effort. Jay had already gotten on the kayak and took the front seat. I aimed to hoist myself up into the back seat but didn't have sufficient leverage from the water. In due course, I lost my balance while partially on board and overturned the kayak! We both toppled into the ocean, and our equipment and belongings were strewn far and wide. Jay retrieved the kayak, paddles and his now-soaked baseball cap; I gathered the underwater camera gear. With renewed motivation, I finally clambered up.

At last I was ready for the dolphins. Yet once on the kayak, I began to notice just how much rolling movement there was on the water. We waited. The undulations continued. Suddenly Jay said, "Hey, is that a shark?" The nausea really hit then. I'm not sure if it was motion sickness or the prospect of being that close to a shark, but I told Jay I needed to get on dry land. We headed back and it took me the better part of the day to recover. Nevertheless, the dolphins are still out there. Maybe I'll get the shot next time.

I look forward to the next time—the next opportunity to hear the island's call and return to photograph this special place, to visually capture all that is so enchanting about Chincoteague, to portray the serenity of the surrounding landscape, the power of wind and surf on Assateague, and the changing nature of the barrier islands.

Countless guts and creeks entwine along Chincoteague's saltwater marshlands.

Last light fades over Chincoteague Bay and the remnants of the Killick Shoal lighthouse (lower left), which once warned mariners of dangerous shoals in the area. Assateague Island, Toms Cove and the Hook are in the distance.

COMMUNITY

Surely few places on earth can rival this tiny island called Chincoteague. Whispers of its proud seafaring heritage echo in the corners of weathered fish houses and across wooden docks jutting into the sheltered bay, before dissipating on a salt breeze. It is a heritage not forgotten by the people who live here. Many still chisel oysters from secret beds or scratch in the pungent mud for a clam supper. Full-time fishermen rise early, beating the sun across inlet and ocean in search of flounder, tuna and sea bass. The rhythms of a centuries-old way of life cannot be denied.

But there are other, newer rhythms here, too. In the mid-20th century, a gold-and-white pony captured the imaginations of millions, with the release of the classic children's book, *Misty of Chincoteague,* and the ensuing motion picture. Soon visitors flocked to the island's Pony Penning made famous by the book, and discovered Chincoteague's other quaint charms.

Nearby Assateague Island has been discovered as well. No longer is the barrier island simply a protecting arm for smaller Chincoteague. Nature lovers visit the national wildlife refuge there to enjoy unspoiled beaches and salt marsh habitats. Today it is one of the most popular wildlife refuges in the nation.

Despite the outside world's discovery of the simple islands off Virginia's Eastern Shore, nothing will alter nature's rhythms. Tides will rise and fall again, and waves will pound the shore in ever-changing patterns sacred to time. Storms will cross the islands on rampages to the sea. The wind will whip the raucous laughter of gulls, and fiddler crabs will skitter across the marsh.

In our fast world, the timelessness of wind, waves and salt air holds immeasurable appeal, and an aging islander bent over a clam rake is an image that is simple and untarnished. This is the allure of the islands and why Chincoteague will always be revisited.

Even those casually familiar with Virginia's seaside are hard-pressed to explain its geography. Only a relative few visitors know the four- to seven-mile-wide finger of land called Virginia's Eastern Shore is a peninsula jutting south from Maryland, its only direct connection to the rest of the commonwealth the eighteen-mile Chesapeake Bay Bridge Tunnel. The Eastern Shore peninsula is bordered on the west by the Chesapeake. On the east, it is protected from the full chop of the Atlantic Ocean by a series of barrier islands. The largest is Assateague Island, which shelters Chincoteague. While the Shore's other barrier islands were abandoned by inhabitants who moved their homes to the mainland or watched them crumble into the sea, Chincoteague has thrived. Thanks to Assateague, generations of islanders have lived and worked just out of the ocean's reach.

None of this is visible to those travelers who know Virginia's Eastern Shore only as a quaint throughway to the Carolina beaches and other points south. But turn off U.S. Route 13, the shore's main artery, and venture a little. Another world unfolds—a world many believe exists only in history books and old folks' memories.

Chincoteague currently refers to an island, but at one time, the name applied to a much larger area. When the first Europeans encountered the bountiful lands around Chincoteague Bay—some historians believe it was in the early 16th century when Italian explorer Giovanni da Verrazzano sailed the East Coast for the king of France—they met Native Americans known as the Chincoteagues. The Chincoteagues' kingdom included the islands now called Chincoteague and Assateague, but historians believe the Chincoteagues did not live there. Instead, written accounts and archaeological evidence show they lived on the fertile banks on the mainland overlooking Chincoteague Bay and the surrounding creeks and marshlands.

The Native Americans knew the entire area as "Chincoteague." Common knowledge asserts the name means "beautiful land across the water," but at least one historian disagrees. According to Kirk Mariner, author of *Once Upon an Island— the History of Chincoteague*, the name comes from a Native American word for "large stream" or "inlet." Mariner asserts 20th century island historian Victoria Pruitt took the name from a 1920's island song, thus popularizing the "beautiful land" explanation.

The Chincoteagues farmed the mainland, moving as necessary to find good soil and plentiful hunting. They frequented the sandy barrier islands to hunt, fish and gather seafood, as well as to collect whelk shells, which they used to make strings of beads for trade. By the late 1600s, most of the Chincoteagues joined the Assateague and Pocomoke tribes on what is now Maryland's Eastern Shore, and white men began to claim Virginia's barrier islands to pasture livestock.

As late as 1872 the mainland area around what

Shanties reflect the island's seafood industry heritage, which boomed until the mid-20th century when over-harvesting and oyster disease took their toll.

Quaint island shops stand along Maddox Boulevard, the island's beach throughway, as well as in the downtown area.

is now Chincoteague was known by that name, too. The post office in the mainland town of Atlantic was known as Chincoteague, while the post office on the island was called Gingotig. Older islanders still remember their childhood elders pronouncing the island's name as "Jingo-tig."

Over the next 100 years, tenant farmers and squatters scratched out an existence, raising crops and cattle on Chincoteague and Assateague land owned by wealthy mainlanders. By the early 1800s, about 200 people, including three free black families, inhabited the two islands. With livestock roaming freely, settlers held periodic pennings to sort and brand animals. The first written account of a pony penning on Assateague appeared in an 1835 letter addressed to a magazine.

The writer, a local man, described the penning as an "ancient custom" that inspired great celebration and attracted crowds from afar.

By the mid-1800s, a shift in ideas and economy was afoot on the islands. Northern cities such as New York and Philadelphia boasted great populations, with the wealthiest among them desiring seafood in a quantity unavailable in that region. As islanders realized they had a remarkably profitable commodity lying virtually at their doorsteps, they quickly shifted from raising cattle to harvesting and shipping seafood, primarily oysters. In just a few short years, Chincoteague grew from a sparsely populated pastureland into a bustling watermen's community. Over the next century, the little island became famous for its "salt

During early morning on sunlit days, wide expanses of marsh glitter as though exposed to frost. Close examination reveals blade edges that are coated with salt crystals, which occur from the evaporation of water conducted through the grass blades. This process rids the marsh grass of excessive salt, although enough remains in a blade to make it taste salty if chewed.

This solitary retreat at
the end of a pier offers rest
and perspective for a
South Main Street
homeowner.

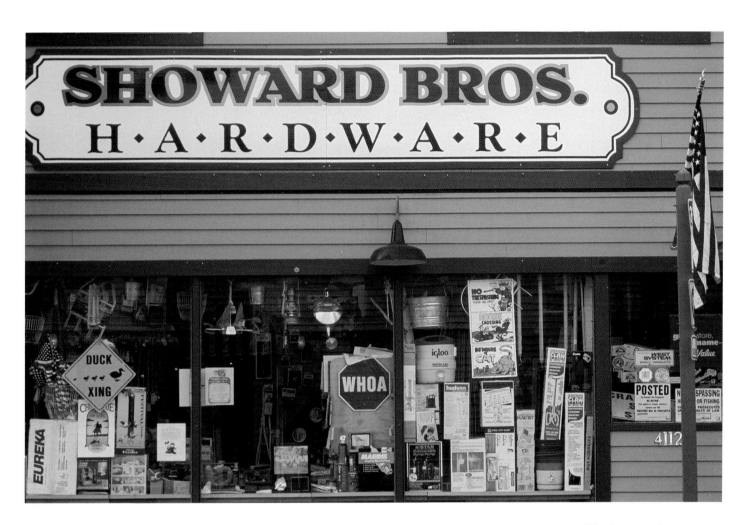

The longstanding Showard Brothers hardware store is a downtown Chincoteague landmark.

Facing: An August full moon rises shortly after twilight. The tip of Wire Narrows Marsh curves toward Chincoteague Island, with Assateague Channel, Horse Marsh, Assateague Island and the Atlantic Ocean in the background.

Above: First light blushes sky and freshwater pools along Beach Road on Assateague. Occasional osprey nests cap the tall loblolly pines, which are the largest and most commonly-found trees on the high dunes that extend along much of the bayside of Assateague.

Above: A chestnut Chincoteague pony mare and her blaze-faced foal graze on lush summer growth on the Assateague salt marsh. The ponies' foaling season generally runs from April through September, with perhaps half the ponies born in May.

Facing: Shadowing the road is the canal left behind by excavations that formed the base of the Chincoteague causeway, which connected the island to the mainland in 1922. The causeway traverses Black Narrows and Wire Narrows Marsh, curves over Queens Sound, then heads toward the mainland in the distance.

oysters," which eventually graced even White House inaugural dinner tables.

For islanders, politics and war were wrapped in seafood industry overtones. When the Civil War erupted in 1861, the rest of Virginia's Eastern Shore sided with the Confederacy. But Chincoteague Island, in a nearly unanimous vote, remained in the Union so as not to sever its oyster industry ties to the North. Several years after the war's end, more change arrived in the form of a railroad connection, which ended at water's edge on the mainland, within sight of Chincoteague. Franklin City, directly across Chincoteague Bay, sprang up at the site and soon visitors transited

Chincoteague Revisited

The Killick Shoal
lighthouse frame prevails
over Chincoteague Bay
waters.

regularly by ferry to the island, some settling permanently in the land of abundant seafood.

With the railroad's arrival, the seafood business became even more profitable. On one Saturday in 1900, nearly one thousand barrels of oysters were shipped to market by railcar. Clams, crabs, and fish also were valuable harvests and several fish factories prospered on Chincoteague. By the 1950s, the island was dotted with a dozen oyster-shucking houses.

The island's boom continued. At the dawn of the 20th century, houses and public buildings, schools and churches, hotels and service businesses were appearing overnight. When the first cars motored onto the island via the new causeway in 1922, the transition from remote island to thriving modern community was complete. But when

Above: A remnant of the once prosperous clamming industry, the Seahawk's *hull is silhouetted against twilit water and sky. Below: Terry Howard (foreground), Chincoteague's longest running councilman, dons moccasins to "wade" clams with his twin brother, Carey. The brothers are native islanders who have worked together in various industries all their lives.*

*Evening motorists
traverse the swing-span
bridge, the island's sole
connection to the rest of
the world, as the tide
rapidly moves through the
Chincoteague Channel.*

the Great Depression hit America in the 1930s, islanders suffered, too. Some supplemented incomes by raising chickens commercially. By the middle of World War II, two million broilers in 130 chicken houses were raised on the island annually. As disease and over-harvesting took a toll on the oyster population, many watermen became chicken farmers. For almost three decades, chickens dominated the economy. By the early 1970s, however, there was no room to expand on the island and Chincoteague growers could not match the capacities of mainland chicken houses. Combined with the devastation of the 1962 Ash Wednesday storm that drowned most of the island's chickens, the broiler industry folded. Chicken City Road continues as a reminder of

the days when chicken was king.

Even earlier, however, a new industry appeared on Chincoteague. Tourism made inroads with the 1876 arrival of the Eastern Shore railroad. Then, in 1947, the island and the fire department's annual Pony Penning achieved worldwide fame with the publication of the children's novel, *Misty of Chincoteague*, and the 1960's movie of the same title. Misty, a gold-and-white Chincoteague pony, was born at Clarence Beebe's ranch on the south end of the island in 1946. Children's novelist Marguerite Henry came to the island that summer to experience the Pony Penning she had heard about from friends. There she met the Beebe family and purchased Misty. The following year, Henry published *Misty of Chincoteague*, the story of two

Waterfront Chincoteague-style houses are in high demand with those eager to own a piece of the island.

Above: Miss Molly's Inn, the birthplace of famed children's novel Misty of Chincoteague, *stands ready to welcome visitors. The inn was author Marguerite Henry's retreat as she penned the Newbery award winner in 1946.*

Facing: Owners David and Barbara Wiedenheft stand in front of the Channel Bass Inn, built in 1892 and housing visitors since the 1920s.

children—based on Clarence Beebe's grandchildren, Paul and Maureen—who want to tame a wild Chincoteague pony named Phantom. At the story's end, Paul and Maureen turn the wild Phantom free and keep her tame foal, Misty.

The story charmed millions and won a Newbery Medal, the highest honor in children's literature. In 1961, 20th Century Fox opened the *Misty of Chincoteague* motion picture, featuring Hollywood actors as well as Chincoteague locals. *Misty of Chincoteague* is still widely read by the young and young-at-heart. Thousands come to Chincoteague each year to see ponies made famous in Henry's book. As a result, and combined with the 1962 opening of the bridge to Assateague's pristine beach and the Chincoteague

National Wildlife Refuge, the island's economic focus shifted from seafood to tourism.

Out-of-town cars crawl the narrow streets in the summer as the year-round population of 4,000 swells to 30,000 for Pony Penning, held the last Wednesday and Thursday in July, when fire company volunteers herd the wild ponies on the Virginia end of Assateague, swim them across the channel to Chincoteague, and auction the foals.

On the last few miles of Route 175, the road connecting the Eastern Shore's main highway to the island, a traveler venturing toward Chincoteague passes the towering radar antennas and rockets of the National Aeronautics and Space Administration's Wallops Flight Facility. Driving past these icons of progress and modernization, it is difficult to imagine what simple

The vintage art deco Island Roxy Theatre was the site of the Misty of Chincoteague *movie premier. The pony's hoof prints were set in the theatre's sidewalk during the premier and remain visible to passersby today.*

pleasures lie just ahead. Suddenly, the road turns and Chincoteague Island is revealed, the outline of modest houses still several miles across vast expanses of marshland and saltwater channels.

Part of Virginia's Eastern Shore, but not touching it, Chincoteague is connected to what islanders call the "mainland" by a thin ribbon of causeway, a four-mile stretch of roads and bridges traversing salt marsh.

With the vehicle window rolled down, a summer's crossing is multi-sensory. A sharp salt tang permeates the slightly sticky air. The pungency of muddy, healthy decay rises and wafts across the marsh. Herons are still, watching for minnows. Mazes of narrow guts, soft tumps and broad patches of cordgrass stretch to the horizon, where on a clear day, vibrant colors merge with the blue-gray water.

Crossing this marshland, the traveler meets Chincoteague Bay. The glitter of sun on water dazzles the eyes as it strains to make out details. Small boats rock gently on the waves. Some boats anchor near the bridges where trout congregate, while other fisherman cast from nearby rocks or bulkheads. Periodically, schools of croaker—so named for the distinctive croak they make—move into the bay. The feisty fish give novice anglers the ultimate fishing experience; croaker bites are fast and furious, their hearty tugs on the bait unmistakable. Other species are common in these waters, including bluefish, spot and sea bass.

But perhaps the most prized fish for eating—and the one that draws anglers to the bay in hordes—is the "flatfish," widely known as summer flounder. The flounder begins life looking and swimming much like other species. But, as it

Above: Island Creamery owner Kelly Conklin demonstrates how to whip up a batch of waffle cones for his homemade fresh-fruit ice cream. On a typical hot summer night, the line of customers reaches out the door.

Below: World-famous Pony Tails taffy is made fresh daily with a taffy-making machine imported from England. The original machine, which is over 100 years old, is on display in the Maddox Boulevard shop.

Katye Allen readies Misty's Black Mist, the great-granddaughter of Misty, for a performance at the Chincoteague Pony *Centre. Black Mist is so gentle she can be ridden with only a string for reins.*

grows older, one eye migrates to the other side of its body. With both eyes on one side, the fish takes to lying on the bottom, cleverly adapted to ambush feeding. The "dead weight" tug of a large flounder on the line is a signal to the angler that a tasty meal may be on that night's supper table.

Other culinary delights thrive in the unseen world of Chincoteague Bay marine life. Chiseled from treacherously sharp beds, plump and salty Chincoteague oysters are ample reward, whether slurped on the half-shell while standing knee-deep in salt water, or steamed later. Clams are another favorite shellfish. Experienced clammers "sign" for them by scratching distinctive "keyhole" openings at low tide. Others drag clam rakes across likely beds, digging with toes at the clink of rake on shell. Locals often "wade clams" by donning

Left: Skylar Reed cuddles kittens saved by the Animal Rescue Coalition, which provides spaying, neutering and other veterinary care for Chincoteague strays, then finds homes for many of them.

Below: The Di Fulvio family, which includes Linda and her daughter, Elizabeth, are "come-heres" who moved to Chincoteague to enjoy the relaxed small-town lifestyle. Linda boards and halter-breaks Chincoteague ponies at Wanna Be Ranch on Ridge Road, which she owns with her husband, Anthony.

Carving decoys is a time-honored tradition on Chincoteague Island. Native Reggie Birch is an award-winning carver who uses only old-fashioned hand tools—a hatchet, a spoke shave and knives made from straight razors—to craft his birds.

Carver Reggie Birch paints a decoy in his Chincoteague shop before aging the surface. Reggie creates works in the tradition of the classic carvers, nonetheless retains a signature style that makes his decoys unique.

The swirling Paratrooper lights the evening sky at the Chincoteague Firemen's Carnival, held annually in July to coincide with Pony Penning.

cloth moccasins and finding the shellfish with their feet, a practice developed by Native Americans.

Not all of the island's bounty is underwater. Dotting the marsh are waterfowl blinds where camouflaged hunters wait, concealed by branches and brush, for winged prey. The coldest, dampest days of winter are ideal for hunting mergansers, black ducks and mallards.

Approaching the island, a glance to the left reveals an odd-looking structure standing in the bay. Few would guess its origins, but the structure once supported a lighthouse in the days before a causeway. Killick Shoal lighthouse, built in 1884, warned ferries of the treacherous shoals lying in Chincoteague Channel. The lighthouse was not a traditional tubular shape, but a two-story house topped by a light. Inhabited by a full-time keeper, the structure inspired local swimming and boating races until the 1922 construction of the causeway eliminated passenger ferries. After the Killick Shoal lighthouse (alternatively spelled Killock Shoals) was dismantled in 1935, a blinking light was affixed to the framework, which remains today.

Just past Killick Shoal, the causeway leads to Black Narrows bridge, opens to tiny Marsh Island, then rises into an old-fashioned steel drawbridge, technically a "swing-span moveable bridge"—symbolic to residents and visitors alike, as the structure connecting Chincoteague to "everywhere else."

The character of an island is embedded in its waterfront, and Chincoteague is no exception. The sturdy watermen's homes lining Main Street and overlooking Chincoteague Bay tell the tale of a hard-working people whose perseverance has lent dignity to their dwellings. The houses, with their plain, two-story facades, eschew wasted ornament and space in favor of practical features like front porches that inspire family and neighborly relations. Though not fancy, these "Chincoteague-style" houses now are sought by buyers eager to own a piece of island history.

On the approach, other facets of island life also are apparent. Massive fishing boats, enormous nets cranked in after a night in search of flounder or sea bass, rock gently against moorings at the fish docks near Main Street. Periodically, a captain signals the bridge-tender. The vehicular traffic stops, the swing bridge yawns wide, and a tall boat glides through. Smaller sport boats zip under the bridge, while flotillas of ducks paddle across

Carnival-goers flock to the stand staffed by The Chincoteague Pony Association, which documents ponies born on Assateague and registers each foal sold at the annual pony auction.

Chincoteague Channel to nibble snails and grass on Marsh Island, only to paddle back again.

The bridge deposits the traveler squarely in the middle of downtown Chincoteague, where little shops and charming eateries bustle with summertime visitors. Miss Molly's Inn, a stately 1886 Victorian on Main Street where Marguerite Henry lived while writing *Misty of Chincoteague*, continues to welcome guests today. Visitors pause to admire Misty's hoofprints in the Island Roxy theater's sidewalk, imprinted at the premier of the motion picture in 1961. The vintage art-deco theater features current films, as well as free *Misty* showings during Pony Penning week.

Also in the downtown district is the Channel Bass Inn, built in 1892 and housing visitors since the 1920s. Today, the innkeepers, who also own Miss Molly's Inn, have established a tradition of fine breakfasts and English afternoon teas. Up the street and around the corner lies the newer Maddox Boulevard business district, that leads directly to Assateague Island and grew rapidly after the bridge connected the two islands in 1962.

Chincoteague Island's long and varied history has produced a unique culture tightly woven with distinct subcultures. Some families have island roots stretching back for generations. Many of the surnames on personal property tax lists 200 years ago are common on the island today—Birch, Bowden, Cherrix, Jester, Tarr, Thornton. These families are so intricately joined through marriage and friendship, and share so many decades of history, that an outsider is never truly one of them. Whether the non-native lives on the island for five years or fifty, Chincoteaguers will usually know him or her as a "come-here," the Eastern Shore term for anyone not native to the area.

Some of the come-heres are young families looking for a better quality of life, but many are retirees from urban areas who have vacationed on the island, some for more years than young native adults have been alive. Often highly educated with successful careers behind them, come-heres are attracted to the area for its rural simplicity, relaxed pace, and relative proximity to family members. Many become active in civic organizations and town government.

Yet another group is tourism-driven, apparent mostly in the summer, and in the spring and fall "shoulder seasons." It is then that everyone who enjoys a vacation home on the island arrives. Every rental house is full, and hotels and camp-grounds are bursting at the seams. Streets and

Facing, top: Island native John H. "Jack" Tarr is not only the proprietor of an electrical contracting business, he is also the town's mayor.
Facing, bottom: Paige and Scott Yoder of Pennsylvania chose the annual Oyster Festival to exchange wedding vows. The couple, pictured holding bowls of oysters, preferred the nontraditional setting because of Paige's family's long history of festival attendance.

Below: Eastern Shore resident Jackie Duncan enjoys the Oyster Festival with her son-in-law and daughter, Milton and Teresa Bunting of Pungoteague.

Above: The Chincoteague Volunteer Fire Company, along with other regional fire departments, *showcases its fire trucks at the annual Christmas parade. Facing: Drummers in the* *Chincoteague High School band march along Main Street in the Christmas parade.*

sidewalks buzz with activity, though most of the faces are unfamiliar to locals.

The last subculture also tends towards transience, but usually over a longer term. Coast Guard Station Chincoteague and Group Eastern Shore are headquartered on the island. A few enlistees hail from Chincoteague where some native families have long Coast Guard traditions, but most personnel stationed on the island are only passing through. The U.S. Navy also has an installation on nearby Wallops Island, and some personnel live on Chincoteague, as do employees of the National Park Service and the U.S. Fish and Wildlife Service who work on the wildlife refuge.

Overall, the subcultures mingle successfully, overlapping in most facets of island life. The natives recognize that the island's economy depends

on its ongoing appeal to come-heres and visitors, who in turn, want to preserve the atmosphere that initially attracted them.

Traditions are important in any small town, and Chincoteague is no exception. Religion is perhaps one of the strongest island traditions and references to God are frequent in everyday life. The number of churches on Chincoteague attests both to the importance of religion, and the differences in ideologies that gave rise to splinter groups. As in the rest of the South, Baptists and Methodists are predominant.

One of the most active organizations on the island is the Chincoteague Volunteer Fire Company. Not only do volunteers respond to fires, ambulance calls and other hazardous situations on and off the island, they also operate the Firemen's

Carnival and Pony Penning each July, and provide year-round care for the wild ponies they own on Assateague. The lives of many dedicated islanders revolve around the needs of the fire company. Often they must leave families and businesses to respond to emergencies, attend meetings, or herd stray ponies on Assateague.

Islanders organized the fire company in 1925 after fires devastated much of the downtown. The fire company took over the annual Pony Penning the same year and held the first carnival to raise much-needed funds. By the next year, the firemen were able to buy a new engine. Since then, the fire company has enjoyed remarkable prosperity, thanks to the fame brought to the island by Pony Penning.

The island tradition of decoy carving likewise

Chincoteague volunteers organized the Island Library in a building that once housed a barber shop. Volunteers serve as the primary staffers of the library.

Chincoteague Revisited

rose out of necessity. Native Americans gave settlers the idea of setting out mock birds to lure waterfowl into landing nearby, and settlers soon learned the more realistically the decoy bobbed in the water, the more game they took home to their families. Over the years, hunters plied various techniques to enhance the float and appearance of their decoys. Some carvers' efforts, known as "shootin' stools," produced better results than others. When old-time decoys began selling for thousands of dollars in the late 20th century, carving for the collector—rather than for the hunter—became the norm. Today, decoy shows and competitions are held all over the country, but nowhere is the tradition stronger than on Chincoteague Island.

Historic downtown Chincoteague is dotted with old-fashioned storefronts.

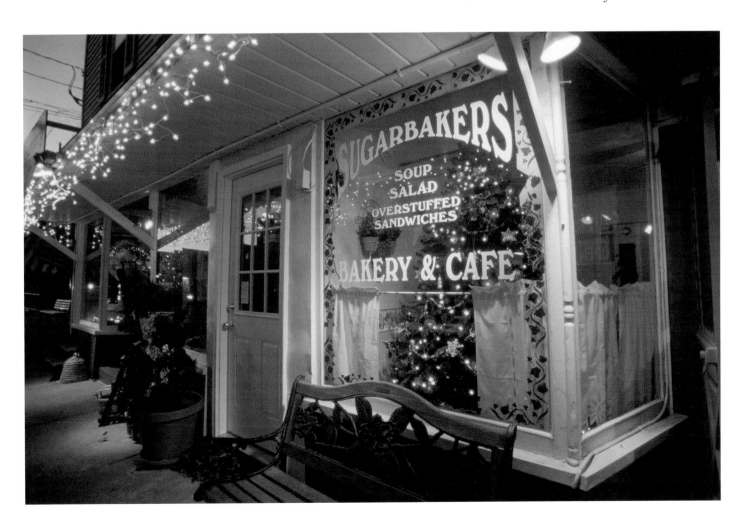

Chincoteague Island comes into view through storm clouds over Chincoteague Channel.

The lengthy docks stretch across the shallows to reach deep water.

Sunset brings a glow to a westerly view of the ocean, Assateague Island and its channel, Morris *Island, Little Oyster Bay, Oyster Bay and the northern end of Chincoteague Island.*

An aerial view of Assateague reveals the effect of sand overwash, *a highly constructive process that is natural to a barrier island.*

REFUGE

The Chincoteague National Wildlife Refuge is a tranquil paradise in a fast-paced world. Pressures and hassles of a modern society are forgotten here. It is a place where herons wait for a meal and painted turtles bask in the sunshine before slipping back into the cool water. Whitetail deer raise graceful heads, ears twitching, before bounding shyly into the pine forest, and snow geese glide across a freshwater pond in serene elegance.

Life is abundant on Assateague Island, which is owned by the federal government and lies in two states, Virginia and Maryland. The wildlife refuge was established in 1943 under the jurisdiction of the U.S. Fish and Wildlife Service to provide habitat for dwindling greater snow geese, which had suffered mightily at the hands of

hunters and through habitat loss. In 1965 Congress established Assateague Island National Seashore to conserve and protect the island for outdoor public recreation. The boundary includes the Maryland end of Assateague, a small portion of the Virginia end, and all of the island's coastal waters up to a half-mile from shore. The national seashore also encompasses Chincoteague National Wildlife Refuge and the 700-acre Assateague State Park, owned by the state of Maryland.

The National Park Service manages recreational use of Assateague beach, while the Fish and Wildlife Service manages wildlife on the beach, as well as the rest of the refuge. Most of the Chincoteague refuge is on the Virginia end of Assateague, while 418 acres are in Maryland, 427 acres are on Morris Island—a marshy area in the

Lush summer growth abounds along the Assateague Channel shoreline, which looks much as it once did to Assateague's first visitors, the various tribes of

Algonquian language stock. These Native Americans seasonally harvested the ocean, estuaries and marshes of the barrier island.

channels and bays between Chincoteague and Assateague islands—and 546 acres are on Chincoteague's northern tip, known as Wildcat Marsh. The refuge also encompasses all or parts of Assawoman, Metompkin and Cedar islands, all lying to the south of Assateague. In total, the Chincoteague refuge—so named because of the refuge system's early practice of naming wildlife refuges after the nearest postal address—includes 14,000 acres of beach, dunes, marsh, and maritime forest.

Undoubtedly, the beach is one of the top attractions for people visiting Assateague. Unlike many East Coast beaches, Assateague remains pristine and unaltered by development. But sunbathing and surfing are far from the only attractions on the refuge. There is biking through

Chincoteague Revisited

maritime forests, horseback riding on the beach, watching birds flutter, dive, and soar by the thousands, and hiking on unspoiled trails rich with natural life. There is something else, too: Serenity—as necessary to happiness as air is to life—and it is abundant on Assateague Island.

At the turn of the 20th century, two dozen cottages, two stores and a school were sprinkled along the west side of Assateague Island facing Chincoteague. Many men of Assateague Village made a decent living by harvesting oysters in nearby Toms Cove, while others worked at the fish factories on the island's curved southern end, known as the "Hook." However, the Field family—John Field, one-time Assateague schoolmaster and physician, and his son, Sam—had begun buying large tracts of Assateague as early as 1891,

The pink hues before a summer dawn envelop the waters of the Assateague Channel along a dock on Chincoteague's East Side Drive.

A September full moon climbs above the Assateague bridge and illuminates the channel and marshes as daylight wanes.

Sunset highlights the remnants of a beetle-damaged loblolly pine forest on Assateague. To prevent and slow the spread of southern pine beetles, refuge biologists perform timber stand improvements such as thinning and prescribed burning. Native hardwood trees, including oak, dogwood and persimmon, are planted to replace damaged loblolly pines and to enhance habitat for wildlife.

Decades of buildup have
wrapped sand around the
old Coast Guard station
(upper left) on

Assateague's Toms Cove.
The station is listed in the
National Historic
Register

The Chincoteague ponies are the result of natural herd selection on Assateague Island. The Chincoteague Volunteer *Fire Company, which owns the ponies, periodically introduces new bloodlines to upgrade the herd.*

mostly from the state. Sam Field, who lived in Baltimore, eventually refused to allow Assateague villagers to cross his property, even hiring an armed guard.

With no safe way to reach their workplaces on Toms Cove, the villagers were forced to abandon Assateague. Many barged their houses to Chincoteague; others simply left them. Today only a collapsed house and a nearby cemetery mark where the village stood.

In 1943, after the death of Sam Field, his sister sold more than 8,000 acres of Assateague to the federal government as a sanctuary for migratory waterfowl. In 1957, after thirteen years of political wrangling between town and federal officials, Congress passed legislation authorizing a

bridge to connect Chincoteague and Assateague. When this bridge opened in 1962, island residents and visitors had access to the ocean for the first time in many years. Though the Chincoteague-Assateague Bridge and Beach Authority originally ran the beach, charging a bridge toll, the National Park Service bought out the authority in 1965. Since then, Chincoteague National Wildlife Refuge has become one of the most-visited refuges of more than 540 in the nation.

The U.S. Fish and Wildlife Service is the federal guardian of the wildlife on the refuge. Though more than a million human visitors visit the refuge each year and the Service makes every effort to accommodate them, the wildlife is the top priority.

Legend holds that the ponies on Assateague descend from the survivors of Spanish shipwrecks, but most historians believe they are the offspring of livestock pastured on the barrier island in previous centuries.

To attract and protect waterfowl, the refuge created over 2,600 acres of freshwater "moist soil management units," or pools. In the spring, biologists lower water levels in the pools to create mudflats, which allow feeding by shorebirds, concentrate the fish for wading birds, and encourage the growth of plants needed by waterfowl. In the fall, rainwater is allowed to build in the pools by closing water-control structures. This provides habitat for migratory waterfowl on Assateague, a vital stop on the Atlantic Flyway used by millions of birds during the fall migration.

The maritime forests also garner attention from refuge management. Much of the forested area fell victim to the southern pine bark beetle after a nor'easter storm covered them in salt spray and caused flooding in 1992. To combat the beetle,

Refuge volunteer Tom Quinn repairs a predator fence with Cassie Brower, a Youth Conservation Corps worker. Volunteers and organizations such as the Youth Conservation Corps are an integral part of the Chincoteague National Wildlife Refuge.

Chincoteague Revisited

A pinto-colored filly stays close to her band. Each band of ponies is protected by a stallion and led by a dominant mare, which determines the group's movements.

*A colt rests in the days
before the annual Pony
Penning roundup when
the ponies are herded to
Chincoteague and the
foals sold at auction.*

Above: The point where the ponies swim from Assateague to Chincoteague is visible at the top left of this aerial view of Horse Marsh and Black Duck Marsh.

Left: Though the Pony Penning roundup is an East Coast affair, the nature of the event is solidly western. The fire department volunteers use traditional cowboy equipment, including western saddles and bullwhips.

The Saltwater Cowboys assemble for the October roundup, one of several throughout the year. There is a long list of riders waiting to join their ranks. All riders must be men from the Chincoteague Volunteer Fire Company or their invited guests. However, the Saltwater Cowboys' duties aren't limited to the glamour of Pony Penning; fence repair, veterinary inspections and mustering strays are among necessary year-round chores.

refuge officials periodically thin and burn areas of the forest, and plant native hardwood trees such as oak, persimmon, and dogwood. Preserving the great forests also protects wildlife such as the endangered Delmarva Peninsula fox squirrel, and non-endangered species such as rabbit, raccoon, fox, whitetail deer and sika deer, a diminutive species of oriental elk introduced to the Maryland end of Assateague in the 1920s.

Another way the refuge manages the area for the benefit of wildlife is the periodic closure of parts of the beach to protect several bird species. One of these is the piping plover, which is

considered threatened. To protect these birds from predation and human interference, refuge officials close the nesting area and provide protective buffers during the spring and summer based on the birds' requirements.

In addition to protecting wildlife, the Fish and Wildlife Service hosts many programs, including bird-watching hikes, marsh walks and children's activities. Visitors throng the island during the annual International Migratory Bird Celebration in May, National Fishing Week in June, National Wildlife Refuge Week in October, and Waterfowl Week in November. The refuge also has an

All eyes are trained on the shoreline as spectators anticipate the return pony swim when the herd is restored to freedom on Assateague. The return swim occurs during slack tide on the day after the foal auction. People patiently await the slack tide and situate their boats along the narrowest part of the Assateague Channel hours in advance.

With only a few foals among them, the Chincoteague ponies take to deep water as they are herded back to Assateague following Pony Penning.

extensive system of volunteers, who do everything from repairing boardwalks and banding birds to helping with Elderhostel programs.

Perhaps the most famous inhabitants of Assateague Island are the ponies. Two herds, separated by a fence, live there. The northern herd lives on the Maryland end. These ponies are owned by the federal government and managed by the National Park Service. According to the Park Service, they are descended from ten horses owned by a seasonal resident of the island.

The southern herd, however, is the stuff of legends. They are known worldwide as the Chincoteague ponies. Though they seem at home on the refuge, the sturdy ponies are not naturally occurring. A popular theory holds that pirates used the barrier island to hide their horses. A still more romantic version of the ponies' origin insists they swam ashore from a wrecked Spanish galleon centuries ago. Most authorities believe the herds descend from stock pastured on Assateague by early settlers. Documentation shows that Chincoteague and Assateague villagers kept livestock on the barrier island. Since at least the 1800s, owners held annual pennings to separate, brand and sell their animals.

Regardless of their domesticated beginnings, the Chincoteague ponies have adapted to the barrier island environment. Small in stature, the ponies survive by drinking brackish water, eating marsh grasses and taking shelter in thickets and stands of trees. Through natural selection, they have developed a stocky build and thick coats to

The herd climbs from Assateague Channel onto Horse Marsh at the conclusion of the return pony swim.

combat the cold winter winds and stinging summer insects.

By nature, the ponies separate into bands, each with a stallion and a lead mare dominating the herd. The bands tend to remain in the same general area each day, foraging for food and water. The size of the band depends on the stallion's ability to defend the mares against other stallions, with a dominant stallion leading up to twenty mares. When a young stallion is successful in stealing mares from another group, a new band is formed.

Unlike the Maryland herd, the Virginia herd's bloodlines have been influenced over the years by outside breeds. Periodically, the Chincoteague

A late-born foal roams the refuge shortly before the October roundup, when pony owners pick up foals they purchased at the July auction but were too young to be separated from their dams.

Chincoteague Revisited

Several miles of trails are available for either hiking or biking. Recreational activities include wildlife observation, photography, education, or simple enjoyment of the outdoors. Approximately half of the refuge's trails are paved while the rest are open to foot traffic only.

Longshore currents sweep sand laterally along the beach, building the Hook at the end of Assateague in this view of *Chincoteague Inlet, Fishing Point, Toms Cove and Chincoteague Point in the background.*

*During the 20th century,
the Hook at the southern
end of Assateague
lengthened by several
miles. Barrier island
sediments are brought in*
*from the shallow
continental shelf, thereby
creating islands,
extending and altering
spits, and curving
peninsulas into hooks.*

Chincoteague Revisited

Volunteer Fire Company, which owns the herd, introduces new breeding stock to improve the size and appearance of the ponies. Consequently, Chincoteague ponies vary in size and coloring. Though most are small, some individuals top fifteen hands (sixty inches) at the shoulder. Colors include bay, black, chestnut, palomino, dun and cremello, with many variations of pinto, or two-toned, coloring.

The herd is kept to a workable size of 150 ponies to prevent damage to the barrier island habitat through overgrazing or excessive competition with naturally occurring species for resources. To maintain the herd's size, the ponies are penned each year and most of the foals are auctioned to benefit the fire company. The event, held the last Wednesday and Thursday in July, is known as Pony Penning.

There is no other experience on earth like Pony Penning. The sheer excitement of modern-day cowboys rounding up colorful herds of wild ponies lures thousands of spectators each year. Countless others watch on television and the Internet as the proceedings are transmitted around the world.

The summer roundup begins out of the sight of most visitors as dozens of mounted "Saltwater Cowboys" search the island for bands of ponies. Braving swarms of summer mosquitoes, they plunge across marshes and gallop headlong through the island forests. Eventually the southern bands break from the woods, their manes and tails flying in the wind. The riders, close behind and shouting encouragement, drive the ponies to holding pens. This process is repeated with the northern bands, which are herded down the beach

Facing: A solitary surf fisherman tries his luck at casting into the Atlantic Ocean. On the sand following the backwash, a shorebird probes for mole crabs, bean clams and worms. Below: Assateague's freshwater pools provide habitat for a vast variety of plant life. Although naturally occurring freshwater wetlands can be found on Assateague, many are more brackish than fresh, and are normally inhabited by plants with limited salt tolerance.

Chincoteague Revisited

the next morning at sunrise. The following days are full of activity. Veterinarians inspect the ponies and their spring foals, deciding which foals are too young to swim across the channel and instead must be carried in trailers with their mothers to the auction on the Chincoteague carnival grounds.

When the day of the swim dawns, the anticipation in the air is nearly palpable. On Chincoteague, about 30,000 people line the shores of Assateague Channel waiting to catch a glimpse of the ponies. On Assateague, the Saltwater Cowboys hang back with the herd until there is no movement in the tides. Then the historic drive is on. With shouts and cracks of their bullwhips, the cowboys drive the ponies toward the channel lined with boats. The ponies, even the young foals,

Facing: The Assateague lighthouse has played a part in the nautical history of the Virginia Eastern Shore since it was erected shortly after the Civil War.

Above: The famous red-and-white beacon, which was originally built at the ocean's edge, now stands far from the water due to the shifting nature of a barrier island. Black Duck Marsh and the Assateague Channel are shown behind and to the right of the lighthouse.

Above: Coast Guard Petty Officer Jesse Rollinger admires the spectacular view from the railing directly below the lighthouse beacon. Visitors may climb the steep spiraled staircase and take in the surrounding landscape from the safety of an indoor viewing area.

Facing, top: The modern lighthouse beacon flashes a unique pattern—a double flash every five seconds—so captains of seafaring vessels will recognize their location along the East Coast. The original First Order Fresnel Lens is on display at the Oyster and Maritime Museum on Chincoteague.

Facing, bottom: It's a long climb to the top, but hardy souls are rewarded by the incomparable view from the lighthouse's peak. The lighthouse is periodically opened for public tours.

are excellent swimmers and frequently swim on their own from one grazing ground to another. As they plunge into the water, the crowds cheer wildly until the ponies hit the Chincoteague shore a few minutes later. After an hour's rest while the cowboys' mounts are barged across the channel, the ponies are herded through the streets of town to the carnival grounds. The sidewalks swell with fans who cheer the cowboys and their charges— especially when a maverick pony escapes to run through residents' yards. Once at the carnival grounds, the ponies are corralled. Visitors hang on the fence to gaze at the animals and to choose the ones they will bid on at the next day's auction, where a strikingly marked foal can sell for several thousand dollars. A few foals are reserved for breeding purposes and are sold to benefit the fire company with the understanding they will live out their lives on the refuge. The next day, the adult ponies and remaining foals swim back to Chincoteague.

The July roundup is by far the most famous interaction between the ponies and the cowboys, but there are also roundups in the spring and fall to inspect the ponies' health, administer vaccinations, and trim their hooves. In the fall, the cowboys separate the late foals that were auctioned in July but were too young to go home with their new owners. Throughout the year, the volunteer firemen check on the ponies and round up stragglers that escape the fences separating them from public roads and trails.

With miles of beachfront, as well as access to marsh and woodland trails, the refuge is a virtual paradise for nature lovers. Red-winged blackbirds cling to tall grasses bobbing in the breeze on the

Biologists manage habitats on the refuge to conserve, restore and protect wildlife and plants. Perhaps the most noticeable management technique is the careful manipulation of water levels in the moist-soil management units. In autumn, water control structures are closed to catch rainwater. The higher water levels provide habitat for waterfowl and other migratory birds.

hard-surfaced Wildlife Loop. During late spring and summer, herons and egrets haunt the freshwater pools around Black Duck Trail, while terns dive for fish. Warblers perch in shrubs as insects keep a constant thrum.

The Woodland Trail reveals the shadowy wonders of forest life as it winds through tall loblolly pines and lower shrubs. Squirrels chatter indignantly at interlopers before scooting up a tree. A glimpse of the shy and endangered Delmarva Peninsula fox squirrel is a rare treat for wildlife spotters. Oriental sika deer, a species of elk released on the island by Boy Scouts decades ago, graze at the path's edge before blending easily into the

undergrowth. From the wild pony overlook, there is a panoramic view of the salt marsh where the southern pony herd grazes.

Another popular path leads to the Assateague lighthouse. The red-and-white striped beacon is a famous sight to seashore lovers and lighthouse fanciers. Like the first Assateague lighthouse built in 1833, the one built in 1867 once stood near the ocean. Due to continuous shifting of sand, the lighthouse now stands more than a mile from shore. This sentinel is much taller and brighter than its predecessor, which stood only forty-five feet high and emitted candlelight. Today's lighthouse stands at 142 feet, and features a revolving

Above: A herd of sika deer, a species of oriental elk, rests on a summer day. Sika deer are much smaller than white-tailed deer and are characterized by their rich brown, often spotted coats. Like the white-tailed deer, sika deer are abundant in refuge woodlands and meadows, and are especially attracted to new, early succession vegetation.

Right: National Park Service guide Gretchen Knapp directs a beach tour, one of many guided activities offered by the Park Service throughout the year on Assateague Island.

light visible for twelve miles at sea. Under the jurisdiction of the U.S. Coast Guard, the lighthouse is open periodically during the year for hardy souls to climb.

All of the refuge's trails offer generous opportunities for birding, one of the fastest growing pastimes in the country. In fact, the island is famed among birders for the abundance and variety of its feathered inhabitants. More than 320 species occur on Assateague, which is set squarely in the Atlantic Flyway, an Eastern seaboard route traversed by millions of birds in the spring and fall as they migrate north or south, depending on the time of year. The migrations are spectacular, as thousands of snow geese and other waterfowl, as well as shorebirds, hawks and falcons, descend on the island to feed and rest.

Eva Savage, an employee of Chincoteague National Wildlife Refuge, surveys waterfowl species to document population fluctuations from year to year. This information is used to determine if refuge goals are being met and to establish the best management practices.

Above: A tourist crabs with his young daughter near Assateague bridge. Most tourists use lines baited with chicken necks to catch the crustaceans, while native islanders generally use baited wire traps.

Facing: Young Emilie is the third generation of her family to spend time on Chincoteague and Assateague islands. For many families, visiting the islands is an annual tradition and a time to enjoy the beach, hiking, souvenir shopping and ice cream parlors.

The shallow waters of Assateague feed not only feathered visitors, but also satisfy the urge of some people to gather their supper from the wild. Crabbing with chicken necks and raking for clams are popular pastimes. On the beach, the possibilities do not end with sunbathing. Surfers and ocean kayakers harness the ocean's waves, which are gentle or tumultuous, depending on the weather. Swimmers take advantage of the salt water's buoyancy while negotiating the tides and currents.

Assateague also offers a unique fishing experience. Anglers can cast a line into the surf, set the fishing pole into a stand, then sit back to bask in the sun, opening an eye occasionally to check

For Chincoteague native
Jay Cherrix, spending
time on the water is as
natural as breathing.

Early on a summer
morning, Jay prepares an
ocean kayak for a ride in
the Atlantic surf.

A child dashes across warm sand on Assateague, one of the most undeveloped beaches on the East Coast.

Though its days of
lifesaving purposes are
long past, the old Coast
Guard station, flanked by
its watchtower, stands on
the southern end of
Assateague as a reminder
of the heroism of those
who saved shipwrecked
sailors' lives.

Chincoteague Revisited author Jennifer Cording rides her Morgan gelding, Saracen, at water's edge on Assateague. For *Eastern Shore riders, a seaside gallop is a favorite Sunday afternoon pastime.*

Fishing Point on Assateague Island's Hook faces Wallops Island. Barrier islands migrate toward the mainland as the sea rises or the coastal plain submerges under the weight of its accumulated sediments. A lifetime is usually not long enough to see the overall trend, but old maps and charts clearly document the change.

Clouds of snow geese rest in pools at the Chincoteague National Wildlife Refuge, a major stop on the Atlantic Flyway. Though the *species once languished because of hunting and lack of habitat, it has rebounded immensely, thanks to effective management.*

the status of the line. Flounder, bluefish, gray trout, kingfish, and several varieties of shark are among frequent surf-fishing catches.

Equestrians ride beside the blue-gray waves of the Atlantic. When the Hook is not closed for nesting birds, horseback riders can follow its edge, riding around the end to the bayside. It's quite a distance, but worth the trip to see the old Coast Guard Station. It is also a mesmerizing way to view expanses of ocean, sand, and inlet, as well as a good vantage to spot dolphin.

Winter grasses on the refuge provide sustenance for snow geese and other waterfowl during cold months.

With the Atlantic in the foreground and Chincoteague Inlet in the background, an April sunset illuminates Assateague's Hook, the old Coast Guard station and Toms Cove.

TRANSITIONS

Barrier island ecology is a study in contrasts. Few forces can rival the sheer intensity of stormy ocean winds and surf, or even the relentless pounding of day-to-day waves. Yet, despite the natural harshness the island continually endures, footsteps on fragile dunes are enough to destroy the grasses, allowing sands to simply blow away. Countless eons of adaptation have equipped barrier island birds with straw-like bills for probing in water, tall legs for wading, or sandy brown feathers for nesting on the beach. In spite of this, human encroachment still threatens their survival. Many species thrive in the island environment, but can be destroyed easily by water or airborne pollutants.

It is a delicate balance. Left alone, nature will maintain this balance. Nevertheless, in awe of the splendor of an island, people at times unintentionally threaten its fragility. Visitors seeking the shortest route to the beach climb dunes and trample the vegetation. A shell-seeker, straying too close to a nesting area, disturbs the parent birds and enables a wild predator to snatch a chick.

Even those charged with protecting the area sometimes have made decisions that altered it unnaturally. Past federal policy of rebuilding dunes prevented natural sand overwash. With each year, however, scientists and everyday visitors learn more about barrier island ecology. The knowledge is passed on, policies change, and those who understand the island act accordingly. Though there remains so much more to learn.

A kayaker among the marshes in the Assateague Channel contemplates the first light of dawn. Kayaks are ideal for traversing salt marshes since they are quiet, easily handled, and of shallow draft.

Chincoteague Revisited

Winter storms build sand embankments on the barrier island beach, while waves snatch heaps of sand and rush them back to the sea. Major seasonal differences in the width and slope of the beach can be observed during summer and winter months.

Sand dunes anchored by sea grasses are vital to controlling beach erosion and are highly vulnerable to human encroachment. Dunes serve as the first line of defense against storm surges, protecting other wildlife habitats from being lost to salt water intrusion. Sand dunes and adjacent areas serve as important nesting habitat for the threatened piping plover and other shorebirds, such as common and least terns, and black skimmers.

Change is the hallmark of a barrier island. Its shape, composition, even its location can never be taken for granted. Always shifting and evolving, the island is reborn with every storm, tide, and sunrise. Perhaps it is this constant change that repeatedly entices visitors to see nature's freshly decorated canvas. Some changes are obvious and regular. Each day the tide removes most signs of human presence and writes a new signature on the shore. Other changes are less noticeable, such as the slow creep of the island to the west and south.

Assateague, one of the major East Coast barrier islands, has been lying at the edge of the Atlantic Ocean for thousands of years, though it once was much farther seaward. Like other barrier

A barrier island's height builds slowly until it eventually reaches an average elevation of about five feet, at which point it is usually stabilized by plants.

Above: The ebb and flow of tides in a salt marsh herald the renewal of life as bacteria break down plant and animal matter into nutrients. The salt marsh plays a vital and often subtle role in the health of bays, estuaries and oceans. Each day brings two high and two low tides, a little over six hours apart. The timing of the tides advances by about an hour a day, since they run close to a twenty-five hour cycle.

Facing, top: The shade cast by high loblolly pines limits the growth of shrubs, therefore the understory in these woodlands is relatively open. Hawks make their home in these trees and the great horned owl is common throughout the year. Facing, bottom: Though best avoided by humans, poison ivy is an important food source for a number of wild species. Similarly, thorny briars provide protection for small animals such as rabbits and toads.

islands, Assateague was formed from sand and rock scoured by prehistoric glaciers and deposited by ancient rivers on the once-exposed continental shelf. As the sea level rose over the millennia and submerged the continental shelf, waves cut into the glacial sediment. The sediment washed closer to shore and eventually formed islands that sheltered small bays and the mainland coast.

Barrier islands are replenished primarily by sand. Longshore currents, which travel laterally along the shoreline, transport grains of sand parallel to shore until waves catch the particles and toss them onto the beach. As the winds blow, and the tides surge and recede, the sands move again, further altering the beach. When windblown sand catches on plants or driftwood, a dune forms.

Chincoteague Revisited

Beach grass grows on the dunes, thus anchoring them. Gentle, steady summer waves build a wide, flat beach. In the winter, however, powerful winds and storms send violent waves crashing to the shore. The waves snatch heaps of sand and carry them out to sea and southward, or throw them across the island, overwashing and building the island's bayside.

Longshore currents not only build an island's face, but also its southern tip. The currents rush along the coast, suddenly falling into the mouth of a bay and depositing sand there. Eventually the sand forms a hooked spit. Assateague's Hook is a classic example of longshore current action. The 1867 lighthouse and the 1920s Coast Guard station once sat at water's edge. Now they lie far inland, thanks to sediment buildup. An early 20th

A spring sunrise paints
the marshes along
Assateague Channel. Yet
in all seasons, marshlands
reveal an austere beauty.

When the tide is out, a
rushing sound can
sometimes be heard even
when the marsh grasses
are still. The source of the

noise is the fiddler crabs,
which swarm to feeding
grounds when the water
level drops.

century fish factory that thrived in Toms Cove on the bayside was forced out of business when sand closed the navigable inlet in the late 1920s. Productive oyster beds in Toms Cove also were ruined when sand shifted over them.

Human management, including the building of dunes and the prevention of natural overwash, has influenced the shape and movement of the island. When storms knocked down Assateague's tall dunes, waves washed away large portions of beach, which were carried southward. Today, the National Park Service lets nature take its course, using only removable bathhouse structures that can be disassembled quickly. Sand is now allowed to wash over the dunes during a storm, naturally moving the island westward.

Scorching summer sun and icy winter winds. The burn of sea spray. Biting insects that pester and torment. A barrier island can be inhospitable. Could life survive here, much less thrive? It seems unlikely, but the barrier island environment hosts an array of life that rivals any non-coastal area. On Assateague Island, more than sixty species of plants exist in the inland ponds alone. Over 300 species of birds occur on the island, and larger mammals such as deer and ponies thrive in numbers requiring careful control to prevent overgrazing.

Still, life and its variations are regulated by the harsh conditions. At the ocean's edge, only the hardiest survive. In the summer, the sun's blazing rays bake the sand. Gulls, terns, and other shorebirds tolerate the conditions, while tiny crustaceans like the mole crab and ghost crab take advantage of cool ocean waves and evening hours to avoid the heat. Few plants attempt life on the beach.

Loblolly pines tower over understory vegetation on a damp autumn day on Assateague Island. The pine woods are excellent for spotting warblers and other small birds, especially during spring and fall migrations.

Occasionally sea rocket or seaside spurge crop up, but merciless conditions usually defeat even these hardy species.

Rising over the beach face are primary dunes. Countless grains of sand catch on organic matter washed in on the high tide, so the dunes are more fertile and support American beach grass. Impervious to salt spray, extreme temperatures and blowing sand, beach grass anchors dunes in most weather conditions. Shorebirds are perhaps the most well known inhabitants of the beach and dune areas. Black skimmers, least terns and endangered piping plovers raise their young in shallow nests of sand. In addition to natural predators such as raccoons and gulls, nesting birds must contend with human influence.

Beyond the primary dunes lies the interdune area, encompassing several smaller habitats. The first habitat is mostly small mounds of sand where milder conditions encourage many life forms. Plants such as beach heather, dog fennel, sheep sorrel, and soft rush live here, as well as ponies, meadow voles, white-footed mice, Eastern cottontails, red foxes and raccoons. Many insects, including relentless greenhead horseflies, deerflies, mosquitoes, and midges, also frequent the interdune area.

Inland from the sand mounds on Assateague are the barren flats, an area created when high dunes are washed toward the bay. Frequent bay flooding prevents establishment of most plants and animals in this area. Next in the inland progression is the thicket zone, where stands of wax myrtle and bayberry are interspersed with greenbrier. Another signature plant is poison ivy, an important food source for many species. Lichens and prickly pear cacti also occur, and small creatures such as rabbits, snakes and toads seek the thickets for protection.

Dotting the interdune and thicket zones on Assateague are a number of freshwater ponds and marshes that mark the rising of the water table in the island's low spots. They are ecologically diverse with dozens of plants nourished by organic sediment. Birds and mammals frequent the freshwater areas. Great blue herons, American egrets and greater snow geese flock, as do vast numbers and varieties of insects. Minnows inhabit the ponds, likely originating as eggs on the legs of waterfowl.

Continuing the westward march across Assateague, a different world emerges in the tall pines. Searing heat is replaced by cool shade, and shifting sands become a soft carpet of loblolly needles. The ocean's timeless waves draw some, but the peace of the forest beckons others. Here the silence is broken only by the chatter of a squirrel, the flutter of a bird, or the whisper of wind in the treetops. Distance protects most of the loblollies from the ocean's salt spray, though storms reach some as the dunes shift and the island moves.

The peace of the forests gives way to the buzz of the salt marsh, Assateague's final zone in the westward progression. Long considered an inhospitable dead zone, in part because of its sulfuric smell and swarming summer insects, the salt marsh is, in fact, the most productive environment on earth. The lifeblood of the island's ecosystem—and of ecosystems far beyond—the salt marsh

The arrival of dawn bathes the loblolly forest and freshwater pools near Beach Drive in a golden light. Egrets and other herons prefer roosting in bayside pines to survey the surrounding waters.

Chincoteague Revisited

Little Toms Cove clears as a September afternoon thunderstorm retreats into the distance. Storms and hurricanes can cause dramatic changes to a barrier island, such as an enormous loss of sand in one area with substantial deposition in another.

Even in places reserved for the wild, humans exert their will over nature. Here, a barrier fence seals the perimeter of Assateague's North Wash Flats, one of several water conservation areas that total over 2,600 acres. A number of refuge habitats are fenced to reduce disturbance by both people and certain wildlife species.

The autumn berries of a Virginia creeper are a valuable food source for refuge wildlife.

filters and breaks down the plant and animal matter washed in by the tide before returning them as nutrients on the outgoing flow. These nutrients refresh immediate and distant environments. Even ocean wildlife benefits from the passing of organic material through the salt marsh.

Additional salt marsh environments exist, such as the estuaries that lie around Chincoteague. These include Black Narrows, Wire Narrows, Shelly Bay and Wallops Neck along the causeway leading from the mainland. Nearby freshwater creeks drain into the marshes, where young flounder and other sea species spend part of their lives.

Locals cite changes to the salt marsh over the last few decades. As a result of snow geese feeding, which grub in the mud and eat tubers and the root systems of water plants, the elevation on the north side of the causeway has dropped. Ponds have formed, and hold too much water for the regrowth of vegetation.

Conventional wisdom once held that salt marsh and other wetlands were useful only if drained and filled. Now ecologists know the true value of these lands. This knowledge has helped spawn a new industry—ecotourism. Many of the area's visitors thirst for knowledge of the natural world they have come to love. Guided kayak and pontoon boat tours of the waters surrounding Chincoteague and Assateague offer a non-intrusive way to learn about the importance of preserving nature.

As surely as the tide rises and falls, the seasons bring change to Assateague. Spring greens the marshes and heralds the birth of new life. Long summer days and sultry nights follow, and the island's lushness matures. Then autumn

Marshlands near Bow Beach off the refuge's north service road give way to the Assateague Channel. Inland bodies of water behind a barrier island are essentially trapped sea water, in contact with the ocean only through an inlet. Salinity levels in the Assateague Channel can be either lower than sea water, due to the runoff of inland rains, or greater if there is little rain and high levels of evaporation from the channel's surface.

Above: For Jay Cherrix, maintaining a simple way of life and championing the value of the natural world lies at the heart of ecotourism. Jay recounts local history and folklore during his *kayak ecotours on the Assateague Channel, and strives to guarantee that area ecosystems are safeguarded for future generations to gently explore and appreciate.*

Facing: Barry Frishman, better known among locals and visitors as "Captain Barry," cruises the Chincoteague Bay and provides fascinating details about the area's history, culture and environment. Passengers on a Back Bay Cruise *might catch crabs by pulling pots, search for marine life on salt marshes and tidal flats, or learn about inter-tidal biology. Captain Barry also tells some great tales about the area's pirates and smugglers.*

Quiet and solitude abound in the moments before dawn on the flat marshes of Assateague Channel.

Chincoteague Revisited

The first light of a summer day presents a landscape in abstract, as viewed from a pier along Assateague Channel.

Overleaf: Verdant high summer marshlands yield to the blue water of Chincoteague Inlet and Toms Cove. The Hook's Fishing Point stretches toward the marshlands, and the Atlantic lies along the horizon.

whispers of inevitable changes, and obediently, island life conforms. Plant life dies back and becomes part of the earth again. Young and old, the creatures of Assateague take stock, then hunker down or move on. Winter descends, and life is hushed, but not stilled—the demands of existence must be met. Then, just as winter exacts its toll, spring arrives again with promise.

It is a cyclic tune the world over, but played out in Assateague's environment, the melody is unique. In this place, the spring and summer mudflats of semi-drained freshwater pools welcome shorebirds hunting for small fish, and encourage nutritious plants for waterfowl. In the winter, the same pools are flooded for migratory ducks, geese and other waterfowl that stop on Assateague to rest and feed before continuing their journey. Wildlife refuge management aids the draining or flooding of the pools when high or low water levels would discourage the

Facing: A rainbow extends over the dunes and across the shoreline following a September storm. Regardless of the season, wave patterns during a storm are not predictable. Waves drive against the shore from every possible angle and carry thousands of tons of sand, rendering wild and disordered seashore landscapes. When the storm subsides, the awesome power of water in motion is manifest along the shoreline. Top: The tawny colors of the nutsedge garnish Assateague's marshes and moist pinelands in the autumn. Nutsedge is beneficial to the area's waterfowl. Above: Bright green leaves of the arrow arum flourish amid the inland pools of the wildlife refuge in early June.

Daily tidal flooding brings nutrients to the salt marsh and makes it one of the earth's most productive natural croplands. Good fishing spots are plentiful along the shore of the Assateague Channel because so many fish wait there for food swept in by tidal currents.

abundance of birds.

Assateague's seasonal changes are echoed on neighboring Chincoteague. Though people out-number wild creatures on the smaller island, the rhythms affect them just as surely. Souvenir-shop merchants close their storefronts in winter's face, as a brisk wind hurtles along Main Street. Hardy birdwatchers visit town on the way to Assateague; locals hustle about their business, minimizing time spent out of doors. Then, just as winter seems to have taken permanent residence, the wind gentles into a breeze, the sky brightens, and the sun-warmed air alerts merchants to open their doors once again. Locals take to the waters, and visitors traverse the greening marshes, cross the island's drawbridge, and Chincoteague bustles anew.

Facing, top: Careful manipulation of water levels is vital in attracting the wide variety of birds and other wildlife to the refuge. Water levels in moist-soil management units are lowered in the spring so that fish are concentrated for wading birds to feed upon, and to reduce plants that are low in nutrition.

Facing, bottom: A great egret displays its breeding plumage. Heron, egret, and ibis rookeries are located on several marsh islands in Chincoteague Bay.

Above: The great egret's wings are proportionately longer and broader than most other white herons and its wingspan can extend over fifty inches. In flight, the great egret holds its neck in a more open S-shape than other white herons.

After a late-summer shower, dusk falls over quieted Chincoteague Bay waters. Up to five miles wide and more than 115 square miles in area, the Chincoteague Bay averages only a little more than three feet in depth. Although relatively shallow, its huge water volume provides a vast habitat for marine life.